W9-BDL-545

## DATE DUE

| | | | |
|---|---|---|---|
| JUN 1 0 | | | |
| JUN 7 | | | |
| JUN 6 | | | |
| | | | |
| | | | |
| | | | |
| | | | |
| | | | |
| | | | |
| | | | |
| | | | |
| | | | |
| GAYLORD | | | PRINTED IN U.S.A. |

# Memorial Day

## By Jacqueline S. Cotton

**Consultants**
Nanci R. Vargus, Ed.D.
Primary Multiage Teacher
Decatur Township Schools, Indianapolis, Indiana

Katharine A. Kane, Reading Specialist
Former Language Arts Coordinator,
San Diego County Office of Education

Children's Press®
A Division of Scholastic Inc.
New York   Toronto   London   Auckland   Sydney
Mexico City   New Delhi   Hong Kong
Danbury, Connecticut

Designer: Herman Adler Design
Photo Researcher: Caroline Anderson
The photo on the cover shows a Brownie Girl Scout placing flags at graves
in a cemetery in Los Angeles, California.

**Library of Congress Cataloging-in-Publication Data**

Cotton, Jacqueline S.
    Memorial Day / by Jacqueline S. Cotton.
      p. cm. — (Rookie read-about holidays)
    Includes index.
    Summary: Introduces the history of Memorial Day and explains how it
is observed today.
    ISBN 0-516-22554-5 (lib. bdg.)    0-516-27369-8 (pbk.)
    1. Memorial Day—Juvenile literature. [1. Memorial Day. 2. Holidays.]
I. Title. II. Series.
E642. C78    2002
394.262—dc21

                                                      2001002683

Do you celebrate Memorial
(muh-MOR-ee-uhl) Day?

## May 2002

| Sunday | Monday | Tuesday | Wednesday | Thursday | Friday | Saturday |
|--------|--------|---------|-----------|----------|--------|----------|
|        |        |         | 1         | 2        | 3      | 4        |
| 5      | 6      | 7       | 8         | 9        | 10     | 11       |
| 12     | 13     | 14      | 15        | 16       | 17     | 18       |
| 19     | 20     | 21      | 22        | 23       | 24     | 25       |
| 26     | **27** | 28      | 29        | 30       | 31     |          |

Memorial Day comes on the last Monday in May. Many people start their summer fun on this day.

They have outdoor picnics with their family and friends.

On Memorial Day, we honor the men and women of America's armed forces who died in wars.

The armed forces are the Army, Navy, Air Force, Marines, and Coast Guard.

8

Memorial Day began
after the Civil War ended
long ago.

America's northern states
fought the southern states
in the Civil War.

Thousands of soldiers (SOLE-jurz) died in the Civil War.

People wanted to remember them. They decorated the soldiers' graves with flowers and flags on a day called Decoration Day.

11

Today, Decoration Day
is called Memorial Day.

People still decorate
soldiers' graves. They also
throw flowers into the
ocean to remember those
who died at sea.

On Memorial Day, a big ceremony (SER-uh-moh-nee) takes place at Arlington National (NASH-uh-nuhl) Cemetery in Virginia.

Thousands of people from the armed forces are buried there.

At the ceremony, the President of the United States places a wreath at the Tomb of the Unknowns (uhn-NOHNZ).

This tomb is a special place
where soldiers are buried
whose names are not known.

18

A bugler (BYOO-gluhr) plays a song called *Taps* to honor those who died for their country.

This song is played at cemeteries, parks, and other places that hold ceremonies on this day.

Another way to honor those who died is to fly our country's flag at half-mast. This means lowering the flag halfway down the flagpole.

Cities and towns have parades.
Veterans (VET-ur-uhnz)
march in the parades.
Veterans are people who
have served their country
in times of war and peace.

Scouts, policemen, and other groups march, too.

Many people visit the Vietnam (vee-et-NAM) Veterans Memorial in Washington, D.C.

This long wall lists the names of members of the armed forces who died in the Vietnam War.

People leave letters, flowers, flags, and other things along the bottom of the wall.

Before you start your summer fun on Memorial Day, take time to remember the men and women who gave their lives for their country.

# Words You Know

Arlington National Cemetery

bugler

Civil War

half-mast

30

tomb

veterans

Vietnam Veterans
Memorial

wreath

# Index

Air Force, 6
Arlington National Cemetery, 14
Army, 6
bugler, 19
ceremonies, 14, 16, 19
Civil War, 9–10
Coast Guard, 6
Decoration Day, 10, 13
family, 5
flags, 10, 20, 27
flowers, 10, 13, 27
friends, 5
graves, 13

half-mast, 20
Marines, 6
Navy, 6
parades, 22–23
picnics, 5
summer, 4, 28
*Taps*, 19
Tomb of the Unknowns, 16–17
veterans, 22
Vietnam Veterans Memorial, 24, 27
Vietnam War, 24
wreath, 16

# About the Author

Jacqueline S. Cotton is a writer. She lives in Idaho with her husband Anthony and son Zachary.

# Photo Credits